SACRAMENTO PUBLIC LIBRARY

D0576193

A TRUE BOOK™

Hillary Clinton

ROBIN S. DOAK

Children's Press®
An Imprint of Scholastic Inc.
New York Toronto London Auckland Sydney
Mexico City New Delhi Hong Kong
Danbury, Connecticut

Content Consultant

James Marten, PhD
Professor and Chair, History Department
Marquette University
Milwaukee, Wisconsin

Library of Congress Cataloging-in-Publication Data

Doak, Robin S. (Robin Santos), 1963–
 Hillary Clinton/by Robin S. Doak.
     p. cm.—(A true book)
 Includes bibliographical references and index.
  ISBN 978-0-531-21906-5 (lib. bdg.) — ISBN 978-0-531-23877-6 (pbk.)
1. Clinton, Hillary Rodham--Juvenile literature. 2.
Presidents' spouses—United States—Biography—Juvenile literature.
3. Women legislators—United States--Biography--Juvenile literature.
4. United States. Congress. Senate—Biography—Juvenile literature.
5. Women politicians—United States—Biography—Juvenile literature.
6. Women presidential candidates—United States—Biography—Juvenile
literature. 7. Women cabinet officers—United States—Biography—Juvenile literature. I. Title.
 E887.C55D63 2013
  328.73092—dc23 [B]   2012036004

No part of this publication may be reproduced in whole or in part, or stored in a retrieval system, or transmitted in any form or by any means, electronic, mechanical, photocopying, recording, or otherwise, without written permission of the publisher. For information regarding permission, write to Scholastic Inc., Attention: Permissions Department, 557 Broadway, New York, NY 10012.

© 2013 Scholastic Inc.

All rights reserved. Published in 2013 by Children's Press, an imprint of Scholastic Inc.
Printed in the United States of America 113
SCHOLASTIC, CHILDREN'S PRESS, A TRUE BOOK™, and associated logos are trademarks and/or registered trademarks of Scholastic Inc.
1 2 3 4 5 6 7 8 9 10 R 22 21 20 19 18 17 16 15 14 13

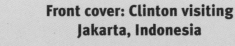

**Front cover: Clinton visiting
Jakarta, Indonesia**

**Back cover: Clinton celebrating U.S. Senate
election win with daughter, Chelsea**

Find the Truth!

Everything you are about to read is true *except* for one of the sentences on this page.

Which one is **TRUE**?

T or F   Hillary Clinton was the first president's wife to be elected to Congress.

T or F   Hillary Clinton was the first female secretary of state.

Find the answers in this book.

3

Contents

THE **BIG** TRUTH!

Life as First Lady

Clinton
campaigning for
the presidency

The Clintons' dog
Buddy was named
after the president's
great-uncle.

Hillary Clinton has been active in the U.S. government for many years.

Early Years

Most Americans first met Hillary Rodham Clinton in 1992. That year, her husband, Bill, ran for U.S. president. She appeared beside him in interviews and at speeches during his campaign. But America soon came to know Hillary Clinton in her own right. As first lady, she advised the president and helped raise their daughter, Chelsea. Clinton also worked for many important causes. After leaving the White House, she carved out an impressive political career all her own.

Bill and Chelsea campaigned for Clinton when she ran for president in 2008.

Young Hillary

Hillary Diane Rodham was born on October 26, 1947, in Chicago, Illinois. Her parents were Hugh and Dorothy Rodham. Hugh was a businessman. Dorothy stayed at home and took care of Hillary and Hillary's two younger brothers, Hugh and Anthony. When Hillary was three, her family moved to a suburb of Chicago called Park Ridge.

Hillary, her parents, and her brother Hugh pose for a family photo.

In sixth grade,
Hillary wrote
a 29-page
autobiography
of her life.

Dorothy Rodham encouraged her children to be
active in their community. She also taught them to
help people who were less fortunate. Even as a child,
Hillary took this lesson to heart. She helped organize
carnivals, food drives, and fund-raisers for groups such
as the United Way. She and her friends even held a
mock Olympics to raise money for charity. Hillary also
took part in church and Girl Scout activities.

Hillary was involved in many activities during high school.

Paul McCartney was Hillary's favorite member of the Beatles when she was growing up.

Changing Values

Hillary was an excellent student who loved learning. From the start, she stood out as a hard worker and as a leader. In sixth grade, she was elected a captain of her school's safety patrol. Hillary was also known as a tomboy. She played softball, ice-skated, and cheered for the Chicago Cubs and the New York Yankees.

In high school, Hillary developed a passion for politics. Her parents were Republicans. At first, Hillary was too. In 1964, she helped campaign for Republican presidential candidate Barry Goldwater. Her opinions changed gradually. In high school, Hillary's teacher asked her to debate from the side of President Lyndon Johnson, a Democrat. When she read Johnson's opinions about issues such as **civil rights** and poverty, Hillary began to consider new points of view.

In her junior year of high school, Hillary was elected class vice president.

Choosing a Path

In 1965, Rodham entered Wellesley College, an all-female school in Massachusetts. She graduated four years later with a degree in **political science**. During her time at Wellesley, Rodham actively supported fairness and equality for all people. She spoke out in favor of civil rights and against the Vietnam War (1954–1975). She also joined the Democratic Party. In 1968, she campaigned for Eugene McCarthy, a Democratic candidate who was also against the war in Vietnam.

Rodham actively supported a number of causes in college that would remain important to her for many years.

Marian Wright Edelman founded the Children's Defense Fund in 1973.

In 1969, Rodham entered Yale Law School in Connecticut. While completing her degree, she worked for groups of people who had no voices in government. These groups included children and **migrant workers**. In the summer of 1970, she was an intern for Marian Wright Edelman in Washington, D.C. Edelman had founded a group that would later become known as the Children's Defense Fund.

CHAPTER 2

A Powerful Partnership

At Yale, Hillary Rodham met an intelligent young law student named William Jefferson Clinton. The two had much in common. They shared a love of law and politics. They were both outgoing and outspoken. Before long, the pair fell in love. It was the beginning of a strong and successful partnership that has spanned decades.

 Bill Clinton attended Yale after studying at Oxford University in England.

Life in Arkansas

In 1973, Clinton and Rodham graduated from Yale. Clinton headed back to his home state of Arkansas to build a political career. Rodham went to Massachusetts to work for the Children's Defense Fund. A year later, she moved to Arkansas to be with Clinton. She took a job teaching law at the University of Arkansas School of Law in Fayetteville. On October 11, 1975, Rodham and Clinton married in a small wedding ceremony.

Rodham did not use Clinton as her last name until 1982.

Rodham smiles with her young daughter, Chelsea.

In 1976, Bill Clinton was elected **attorney general** of Arkansas. That year, Rodham joined the Rose Law Firm, one of the oldest law partnerships in the United States.

Clinton was elected governor of Arkansas in 1978. In the coming years, Rodham balanced being the state's first lady with many other activities. In 1979, she was made a partner in the Rose Law Firm. Then in 1980, she gave birth to a daughter, Chelsea Victoria.

The Clinton family makes its way to a ball celebrating Bill's election as governor in 1987.

Clinton spent 12 years as first lady of Arkansas. During that time, her husband relied on her for advice and help. When he formed a special education committee, he made her the chairperson. She helped found a statewide organization to aid children and families. She also served as an adviser to the Children's Defense Fund and other children's aid groups. In 1983, she was named Arkansas Woman of the Year.

Chelsea Clinton

Chelsea Clinton grew up in two very famous houses. Her early years were spent at the Governor's Mansion in Little Rock, Arkansas. Her teen years were spent in the White House. When her dad left office, Chelsea was 20 years old. Since then, she has earned bachelor's and master's degrees, gotten married, and worked as a television reporter. In 2008, Chelsea campaigned for her mother when Clinton ran for president.

Campaigning for President

In 1992, Bill Clinton decided to run for president of the United States against sitting president George H. W. Bush. Hillary Clinton was with her husband every step of the way. She campaigned day and night. She traveled across the nation to persuade voters to support her husband. She spoke to audiences of all

sizes and appeared on television beside him. Her father and brothers also took to the campaign trail.

Bill Clinton participated in debates with Republican candidate George H. W. Bush (left) and Independent Ross Perot (right).

When campaigning, Bill said that a vote for him was a "twofer"—two leaders for the price of one.

Campaigning was not always easy. Clinton was asked many personal questions about her life with her husband. Some people criticized her for being too outspoken and independent. With a successful career of her own, Clinton didn't fit the mold of many former first ladies. Critics worried that she would be too involved with decision making in the White House. Others even criticized her hairstyles. Could voters accept this strong first lady?

Bill Clinton raises his hand as he takes his oath of office in 1993.

CHAPTER 3

First Lady

On November 3, 1992, Americans went to the polls to choose their next president. Bill Clinton easily won the election. On January 20, 1993, he was sworn in as the 42nd president of the United States. Hillary Clinton held the Bible used for the swearing in. The new president already had a job in mind for his wife. It would be very important and would thrust the new first lady into the national spotlight.

 In 1993, Bill Clinton was sworn in on a Bible that was given to him by his grandmother.

Hard at Work

After the family moved into the White House, Hillary Clinton went right to work. She was the first first lady to set up her office in the building's West Wing, where the president had his offices. Previous first ladies had always worked from the East Wing. Clinton surrounded herself with a staff of smart, hardworking people. Her office soon became known as Hillaryland.

Clinton immediately started work in support of many of her favorite causes as first lady, including education and children's rights.

24

Clinton was the third first lady to testify before Congress.

Clinton was appointed leader of the newly created President's **Task Force** on National Health Care Reform. In this job, she interviewed medical and insurance professionals. She talked to people affected by rising medical costs. She looked for ways to improve the health care system. Clinton **testified** about the group's findings and a suggested plan of action before Congress in September 1993. Critics argued the new health care plan was too complicated and costly. The plan was eventually abandoned. But Clinton would continue to fight for health care and children throughout her career.

Clinton traveled to many countries around the world as first lady.

Clinton was an active first lady. She sometimes attended the president's morning meetings with his senior staff. She continued speaking out for better health care for American children, women, and veterans. She held conferences at the White House to discuss school violence and other important topics. She also traveled all over the world, representing her husband and the nation. She was especially interested in how women were treated in other countries.

It Takes a Village

Since her college days, one of Clinton's favorite causes has been the well-being of children. In 1996, the first lady published a book called *It Takes a Village: And Other Lessons Children Teach Us*. It talked about her vision for a nation that took care of all its children. The book was a best seller. Clinton toured the country and appeared on television to talk about it.

Tough Times

Clinton faced several difficult times during her husband's eight years in office. In 1994, she had to face questions about her role in a business scandal known as Whitewater. She was called to testify in front of a **grand jury**. The grand jury found no evidence that Clinton had broken the law. Then in 1998, she stood by the president as he publicly admitted to having a relationship with another woman.

Clinton held press conferences and spoke in front of a grand jury in defense of her role in Whitewater.

Clinton was the first first lady to run for public office.

What's Next?

As her second term as first lady came to a close, Clinton began to think about life after the White House. In 1999, the Clinton family bought a house in Chappaqua, New York. A short time later, Clinton announced that she wanted to become New York's next U.S. senator. To represent the state, she needed to be a resident. With this in mind, she moved out of the White House and into the Chappaqua home.

Life as First Lady

As first lady, Hillary Clinton balanced many different roles.

Mother
Clinton's top priority was making sure that Chelsea was healthy and happy. She and her husband kept their daughter out of the spotlight as much as possible.

Assistant to the President
In her West Wing office, Clinton kept up-to-date on political issues. She acted as an unofficial adviser to the president, and he valued her opinions highly.

Hostess at the White House

The first lady entertained important politicians and famous figures from around the world. She held dinners, balls, teas, and Easter egg hunts. She even hosted a gathering of former first ladies.

Patron of the Arts

Clinton helped found Save America's Treasures. This federal group helped protect the nation's historic buildings and artwork. She also started the first White House Sculpture Garden. It featured works by American artists.

World Ambassador

Traveling around the world, Clinton was a spokesperson and ambassador for the president. She was never afraid to speak her mind. In 1995, the First Lady spoke out at a United Nations meeting in China about the treatment of women in that country and around the world.

Clinton and her daughter Chelsea celebrate after learning Clinton had won the senate election in 2000.

Making Her Own Mark

In January 2001, Clinton returned to Washington, D.C., as the **freshman senator** from New York. She had defeated her Republican opponent by gaining 55 percent of the vote. The election was a historic one. Clinton was the first first lady to be elected to public office. She was also the first woman elected to represent the state of New York in the U.S. Senate.

 For 17 days, Clinton was both the first lady and a U.S. senator.

Senator Clinton

Eight months into Clinton's first term in the Senate, terrorists attacked the United States. After the September 11, 2001, attacks, she helped secure $21 billion in aid to help New York City recover. She later traveled to Iraq and Afghanistan to visit U.S. troops there. The new senator also continued to fight for her favorite causes, including health care and children.

Clinton visited troops and toured military barracks in Iraq and Afghanistan as a New York senator.

Clinton was the first New Yorker ever appointed to the Senate Armed Services Committee.

SEN. CLINTON

Senator Clinton was popular with the people of New York. In 2006, she was reelected to the Senate. She received almost two-thirds of all the votes cast. During her second term, she worked to bring an end to the Iraq War (2003–2011). She also supported plans to help Americans who were suffering as the U.S. economy worsened.

In 2007, Clinton announced her presidential campaign on January 20, the date that presidents are sworn into office.

The First Woman President?

In early 2007, Senator Clinton announced that she would run to become the first female president of the United States. Clinton quickly began her campaign. She crisscrossed the nation, talking to voters about her years of experience and her many accomplishments. She also took part in debates with other Democratic candidates. Only one Democratic candidate could run for president. Clinton had to prove she was the right one for the job.

A series of elections took place to determine which Democratic candidate would run. By the spring of 2008, two candidates stood out from the rest. They were Clinton and Illinois senator Barack Obama. By June, though, Clinton had fallen behind. At the Democratic National Convention in August, she gave a passionate speech urging her supporters to now give their support to Obama. Obama was named the Democratic candidate for president, and Clinton energetically campaigned for him.

Clinton gave a speech in support of Barack Obama's campaign at the Democratic National Convention.

CHAPTER 5

Madam Secretary

In November 2008, Barack Obama was elected the first African American president of the United States. Soon after, he chose Clinton to be his secretary of state. The secretary of state is one of the most important positions in government. It is the secretary's job to travel around the world and work with the leaders of other nations. The secretary is the president's top adviser on all international issues.

Clinton was the third female secretary of state, after Madeleine Albright and Condoleezza Rice.

Working for the President

One of Clinton's first acts as secretary of state was to telephone leaders around the world. She talked to them about her and President Obama's vision for international cooperation. Over the coming months, she flew around the world to meet with these leaders. In some places, she hammered out trade agreements. In other nations, she helped smooth and strengthen relations with the United States.

Timeline of Secretary of State Clinton's 2012 Travels

January

Clinton visits Liberia, Côte d'Ivoire, Togo, and Cape Verde in Africa to support peace and economic improvement in those nations.

February

Clinton meets the leaders of seven nations, including Germany, Bulgaria, and Mexico.

As secretary, Clinton worked to make the State Department stronger and more important. She also continued to focus on issues that were important to her. She was an **advocate** for women and children in the United States and around the world. In a speech to the United Nations, she boldly spoke out in support of gay rights. She also created a plan to help ease hunger around the world.

April

Clinton visits South America, where she speaks at events in Colombia and Brazil. She also visits Belgium for a NATO meeting and travels to France and China.

May

Clinton travels to India, then heads home for an important international meeting in Chicago, Illinois, to discuss future interactions among nations.

June

Clinton visits 13 nations, including Denmark and Turkey. In Sweden, she meets with officials to discuss green energy and other topics.

What's next for Hillary Rodham Clinton? In early 2012, Clinton announced that she would not continue as secretary of state if President Obama were reelected. She has said that she would continue to fight for women, children, and health care reform. Many Americans hope that in 2016 Clinton will run again to be president of the United States.

Clinton was named one of the most powerful women in the world by Forbes magazine while in Obama's cabinet.

Clinton worked hard during her four years as secretary of state.

During her last year as secretary, Clinton told her friends that she had never worked harder. Perhaps she will retire from politics and take a much-deserved break from public life. Those who know Clinton, though, believe she won't remain inactive for long.

Whatever she chooses to do, it will be done with hard work and determination, as has been the case for all of her career. ★

Date of Clinton's birth: October 26, 1947

Name of Clinton's parents: Dorothy Howell (1919–2011) and Hugh Ellsworth Rodham (1911-1993)

Colleges Clinton attended: Wellesley College, Yale Law School

Name of Clinton's husband: William Jefferson Clinton (1946–)

Name of Clinton's daughter: Chelsea Victoria (1980–)

Government positions Clinton has held: U.S. senator from New York, U.S. secretary of state

Titles of Clinton's publications: *Dear Socks, Dear Buddy: Kids' Letters to the First Pets* (1998); *It Takes a Village: And Other Lessons Children Teach Us* (1996); *An Invitation to the White House: At Home with History* (2000); *Living History* (2003)

Did you find the truth?

T Hillary Clinton was the first president's wife to be elected to Congress.

F Hillary Clinton was the first female secretary of state.

Resources

Books

Bausum, Ann. *Our Country's First Ladies*. Washington, DC: National Geographic, 2007.

Eagan, Jill. *Hillary Rodham Clinton*. Pleasantville, NY: Gareth Stevens, 2010.

Guernsey, JoAnn Bren. *Hillary Rodham Clinton: Secretary of State*. Minneapolis: Twenty-First Century Books, 2010.

Landau, Elaine. *The President, Vice President, and Cabinet: A Look at the Executive Branch*. Minneapolis: Lerner Publishing Group, 2012.

Visit this Scholastic Web site for more information on Hillary Clinton:
★ www.factsfornow.scholastic.com
Enter the keywords **Hillary Clinton**

Important Words

advocate (AD-vuh-kit) — a person who supports an idea or plan

attorney general (uh-TUR-nee JEN-ur-uhl) — the top law officer of a country or state

civil rights (SIV-uhl RITES) — the individual rights that all members of a democratic society have to freedom and equal treatment under the law

freshman senator (FRESH-muhn SEN-uh-tur) — someone in the first year of service as a senator

grand jury (GRAND JUR-ee) — a group of people who meet to decide if there is enough evidence to try someone for a crime

migrant workers (MYE-gruhnt WUR-kurz) — people who travel from one place to the other looking for work

mock (MAHK) — imitation; not real

political science (puh-LIT-i-kuhl SYE-uhns) — the study of governments and how they are run

task force (TASK FORS) — a group formed for a limited period of time to deal with a specific problem

testified (TES-tuh-fyed) — stated what you have witnessed or what you know

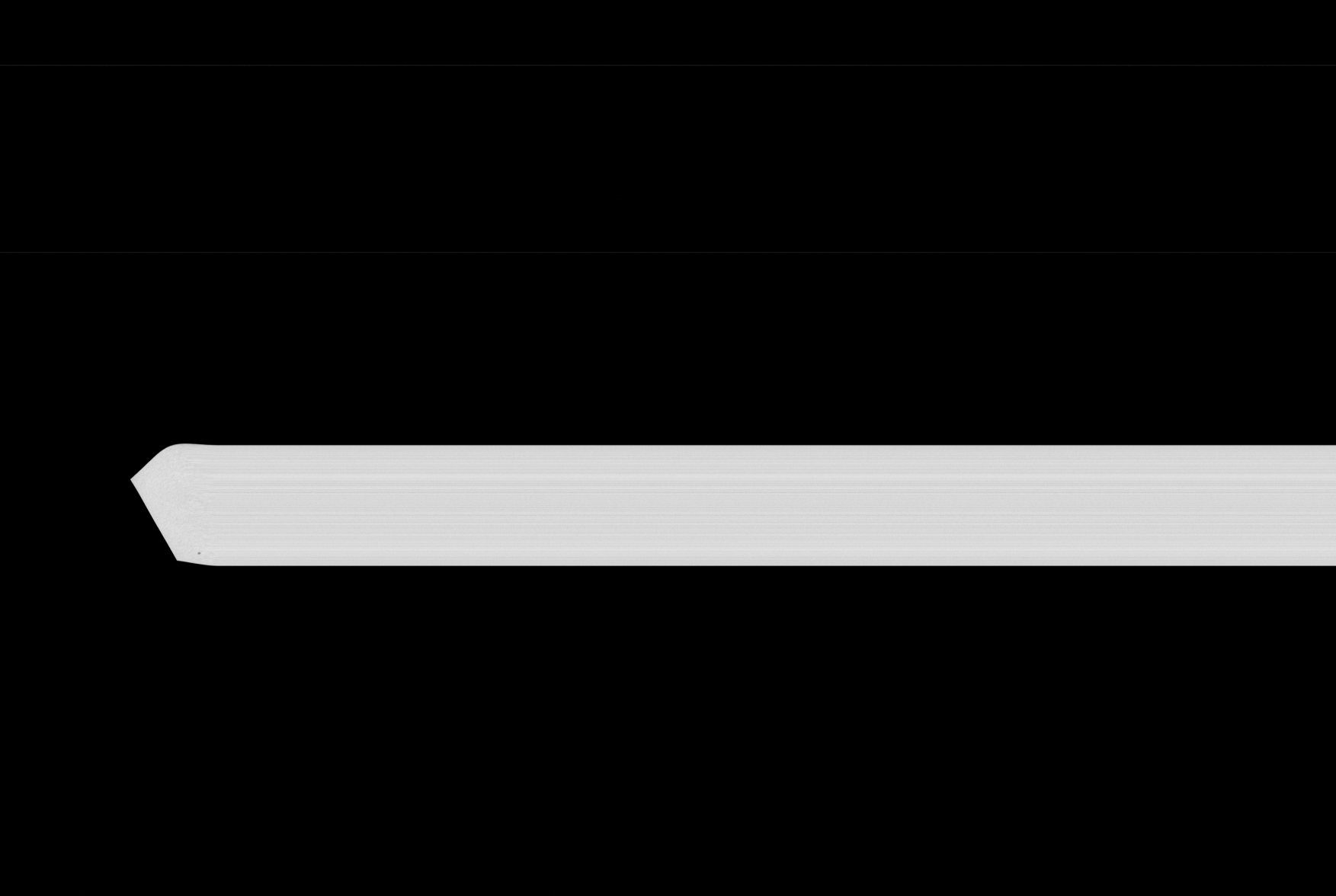

Index

Page numbers in **bold** indicate illustrations.

About the Author

Robin S. Doak has been writing for children for nearly 25 years. A graduate of the University of Connecticut, Robin loves writing about history makers from both the past and present. She lives in Maine with her husband, two dogs, and a cat named Lumpy.

PHOTOGRAPHS © 2013: Alamy Images: 40 (epa european pressphoto agency b.v.), 24 (Richard Ellis), 5 top, 36 (Ronald Karpilo); AP Images: cover (Achmad Ibrahim), 25 (Doug Mills), 41 left (Evan Vucci), 43 (Haraz N. Ghanbari), 31 bottom (Jerry McBride, The Durango Herald), 31 top (Marcy Nighswander), 19 (Matt Rourke), back cover, 32, 44 (Ron Edmonds), 20 (Scott Applewhite), 11; Corbis Images: 13 (Bettmann), 27 (Ira Wyman/ Sygma), 17 (Mike Stewart/Sygma), 3, 6 (Stephanie Sinclair/VII), 12, 18 (Sygma); Dreamstime: 30 background, 31 background; Everett Collection/Ron Sachs/Rex USA: 35; Getty Images: 21 (Cynthia Johnson/Liaison), 28 (Diana Walker/Time Life Pictures), 41 center (Sanjeev Verma/Hindustan Times); iStockphoto/John Moore/ EdStock: 37; Landov: 34 (Dusan Vranic/Reuters), 38 (Jonathan Ernst/Reuters), 5 bottom, 30 foreground (Larry Downing/Reuters), 41 right (Tim Brakemeier/DPA), 26 (Win McNamee/Reuters); Superstock, Inc.: 22 (Everett Collection), 29 (Visions of America); The Granger Collection/Rue des Archives: 10, 14; White House Photo/Pete Souza: 42; William J. Clinton Presidential Library: 4, 8, 9, 16.